Practical Strategies and Tools for Educators

by Susan M. Hentz & Phyllis M. Jones

Council for Exceptional Children
Arlington, Virginia

Council for Exceptional Children
2900 Crystal Drive, Suite 1000
Arlington, VA 22202
www.cec.sped.org

Library of Congress Cataloging-in-Publication data

Hentz, Susan M.
Collaborate smart: Practical strategies and tools for educators / by Susan M. Hentz and Phyllis M. Jones.
p. cm.
Includes biographical references.

ISBN 978-0-86586-464-1 (soft cover edition)
ISBN 978-0-86586-492-4 (eBook edition)

Book design by Sheila Sons, She Designs, Inc.

Printed in the United States of America by AGS.

First edition

10 9 8 7 6 5 4 3

Contents

Our Dedications

Susan

To my extended family from young to old:
Paige, Brooke, Michael, Bradley, Donnie, Ryan, Alyssa,
Jeanne, Lisa, Bobby, Donnie, Kathy, and Mom
for all of the years of practice in my communication
and collaboration skills. Our times of laughter are endless.

Additionally, this book is dedicated to the memory of my father,
Donald George Hentz, who passed during this collaborative process.
He always had something to say about everybody with
his caring heart and priceless sense of humor.

Phyllis

To the four men in my life from young to old:
Sammy, Josh, Zach, and Bill, who epitomize the joy
of communication every day.

Additionally, I dedicate this book to my sister, Lynne,
who during the writing of this book supported me through a major
health challenge by always being there for me. Thank you, Lynne.

Susan and Phyllis

This book is dedicated to the thousands of professional
and personal circles of support who have enhanced the quality
of our lives as educators. It is also dedicated to each and every one
of you. May you continue to grow as positive collaborative partners!

Acknowledgements

We wish to thank the students, educators, and outstanding professionals that have been part of our consultative, collaborative, and co-teaching experiences. We hope the contents of this book will empower you with the strategies and tools to support you to surpass your potential as a collaborative partner.

Numerous people have read our transcript and have inspired us with valuable input and support to persevere throughout this process. Our sincere appreciation is extended to each and every one of them. First and foremost, we are especially grateful that Stefani Roth, CEC Director of Publications, was part of this process. Her feedback, support, sense of humor, and attention to fine detail has encouraged us throughout this journey. Also, Dr. Lynn Boyer in appreciation of her collaborative support and efforts in connecting us as educators with the voice and vision of special education for the Council for Exceptional Children.

Our good friends have been an important part of this collaborative endeavor in so many ways. A special thank you to Sheila Sons of She Designs Inc. for sharing her enthusiasm, friendship, and support in formatting the book and designing the cover. We also want to celebrate personally the following individuals for their invaluable contributions in the reviewing process: Judy F. Carr, Linda Daniel, Jack Griff, Pam McCurdy, Nancy Mills-More, Stacy Straus, Jeff Weller, Julia White, and Bill & Niki Wood for proofreading the copy while offering expert suggestions for improving the book. Thank you for your professionalism and continued modeling of true collaboration and friendship.

Preface

While planning and writing *Collaborate Smart: Practical Strategies and Tools for Educators*, the authors consulted and collaborated throughout the process. This afforded a practical opportunity to incorporate the authors' different backgrounds and perspectives on the principles of collaboration, effectively reinforcing the very practices outlined herein. The result is a book—and a collection of consulting and collaboration "how tos" and checklists—that is different from what we each would have written individually.

Throughout this book, we refer to key strategies and tools within the context of three types of educational relationships: collaborative, consultative, and co-teaching. Writing this book collaboratively illustrated the important elements of collaborative practice and allowed us to reflect on our own skills and attributes.

The evolving process of our collaboration involved negotiation, re-negotiation, respect, trust, and the creation of a level of comfort in our partnership that allowed for risk taking in thinking and practice. This book is a result of the fusion of two sets of ideas and experiences regarding collaboration.

Achievement is a we thing, not a me thing,
always the product of many heads and hands.

J. Atkinson

Introduction

A book focusing on collaborative practice is a welcome addition to the resource kit of today's educators. Federal legislative policies translate into requirements at the state level. Educators face mandates to meet the needs of all learners in the general education classroom, resulting in significant shifts in roles and responsibilities. Students with diverse learning preferences, styles, interests, strengths, and needs are expected to reach certain levels of proficiency in English, language arts, math, and science curriculum standards. One of the biggest challenges for educators is to assist all students to succeed in meeting the demands in the general education curriculum. Many schools have moved toward increased collaborative practices to meet the challenges of the mandated requirements that directly affect state and local expectations in schools.

The current day-to-day work of teachers is influenced more than ever by the defining contexts of research-based best practices. Many teachers are sharing responsibility in creating and sustaining small, flexible, dynamic learning environments that incorporate current best practices in effective and collaborative partnerships across states, districts, schools, and classrooms. Current legislative initiatives have mandated the implementation of evidenced-based practice.

An example of an evidence-based practice, the response to intervention (RTI) model, provides high-quality instruction based on data to make collaborative educational decisions. This multilevel, systematic method for providing high-quality instruction and a three-tiered model of interventions is matched to student need. One of the main advantages of an RTI model is the emphasis on ensuring appropriate learning opportunities for all students, beginning in the general education classroom (Johnson & Smith, 2008, p. 42). The crucial features of RTI include universal screening, collaborative problem solving, implementation of research-based interventions, and data-based decision making.

Teachers collaborate with a myriad of professionals at different levels to improve teaching and learning outcomes for their students. Differentiating instruction, partnering, and co-teaching provide practical strategies to foster dynamic teaching and learning environments involving planning, instruction, evaluation, and reflection. In an era requiring increased accountability and progress monitoring, collaborative teaching models can result in more schools making adequate yearly progress at the elementary, middle, and high school levels. Working with other education professionals may be short term, but also more intense, which requires nurturing and negotiation at the systemic level. Collaborating with students, parents, and paraprofessionals should be an ongoing process with continuous professional and sensitive management and evaluation.

This book translates principles into actual classroom practices by providing strategies and tools for effective collaborative practice. Teachers can apply the tools presented in this book to any level of collaborative work across classrooms, schools, districts, and organizations. **Chapter 1** focuses on the fundamental principles of collaboration from the practice of consultation to shared teaching. The principles of effective communication and the importance of developing a mutual understanding of collaborative endeavors are central to this chapter. Reflective practice is presented as an essential means of strengthening collaboration. Administrative "buy in" for the support of the collaborative can influence the success of the project. **Chapter 2** identifies many practices that foster teams working better together. Personal attributes, roles, and responsibilities (individual and group), and approaches to maintaining group structures are key components in the creation of successful teams. Team maintenance and conflict management strategies are discussed as important factors in teaming. **Chapter 3** addresses the nature, practices, and underlying structures of collaboration. Personal qualities, preferences, and collaborative roles and responsibilities contribute to the ultimate effectiveness of any partnership. Informed planning for collaboration is presented, along with implementation tools that identify activities and responsibilities that facilitate collaboration. Delegation is promoted as an effective means for sharing responsibilities, with the level of success influenced by mutual agreement on the delegated task and the expected outcomes. **Chapter 4** focuses on the identification of partners and their contributions based on the issue or the need for the consultation. Tools and strategies are introduced to support the process from the initiation to the evaluation. These relate to the identification of key support personnel, the area of need for support, requesting support, managing information, and evaluation. **Chapter 5** presents co-teaching as the ultimate collaborative practice that demands careful planning, implementation, and evaluation. Various co-teaching partnerships and approaches are discussed. Tools and strategies are introduced that enhance the practice and evaluation of co-teaching. Throughout the book, the number of practical tools and strategies becomes increasingly greater within the continuum of effective partnerships.

CHAPTER ONE

*"True communication is an open bridge that works both ways.
When we build bridges, we can keep crossing them."*

Jane Alvarez

The Fundamentals of Collaboration

The effective application of consultation, collaboration, and co-teaching can improve achievement of students with diverse learning strengths and needs due to varying ability, culture, gender, and socioeconomic status. The current trend toward collaboration in education is supported by evidence-based research that increases student outcomes (Marzano, Pickering, & Pollock, 2001). Fundamental principles apply to all partnerships, and serve as practical and vivid indicators of the successes and effectiveness of the collaboration. The tools and strategies that nurture collaborative practices are essential components. Effective communication combined with the principles of trust, respect, and research-based practices provide a forum for educators to engage in professional development. This positively affects the ability to apply the strategies of consultation, collaboration, and co-teaching.

Communication Skills

Communication is the verbal or nonverbal exchange of information, meaning, and feelings. It incorporates every possible way we interact with each other. Communication skills are a component of all relationships; therefore it is a good return on investment to spend time developing and improving the communication process. Effective communication occurs when the message sent by one person is received as intended by others.

Listening involves a receiver and sender of information and includes non-verbal language such as eye contact, gestures, posture, and affirming the speaker through nods and smiles. This illustrates active listening and prompts increased understanding of the topic. Listening is the foundation of communication, and this skill can improve with practice. Reflect for a moment on the impact of listening, talking, and responding to others in a recent collaborative interchange. *What went well? What didn't? Would the interchange have been more effective if attention to listening skills occurred?* People speak at 100 to 175 words per minute, but they can listen intelligibly at up to 300 words per minute. From the listener's perspective however, it is easy to drift from a conversation, underscoring that active listening is an absolute necessity in positively influencing two-way communication. An effective listener

- reflects and is nonjudgemental.
- respects silences to aid in processing of information.
- shows enthusiasm in hearing the other person's point of view.
- values the fact that the other person "owns" the issue.
- summarizes or paraphrases information received.

Personal judgments, beliefs, and assumptions can distort the meaning of what is said, so it is important to be sure there is a mutual understanding of the actual message being received. For example, an effective listener may use the following phrases: "You seem to be saying that..." or "Am I correct in hearing you say ... "I understand that..."

As the receiver in the communication process, the role is to listen to colleagues, accurately paraphrase the message, and validate the information. As the sender in the communication process, the role is to share the message, help with clarification, and acknowledge the receiver understands the information. Listening and responding in a way that respects differences and acknowledges all contributions is crucial. Barnitt (2006) offers a range of probing questions to facilitate in-depth conversations about the practice. An example of a probing question is "Why have you always done it like this?"

Good communication skills require a higher level of self-awareness to gain an understanding of personal styles of communication. **Tool 1.1, Communication Checklist** (p. 7), identifies areas of strength and needs in communication skills that are important components for successful

Communication Checklist

Name:

Directions: Read each prompt and assess your current communication skills. Place a check mark in the appropriate column. N = Never S = Sometimes A = Always

Communication Skill	N	S	A
Do you determine the mood of others by looking at their non-verbal cues?			
Do you check your nonverbal messages? (e.g., facial expressions)			
Do you give appropriate eye contact?			
Do you actively listen?			
Do you smile?			
Do you interrupt the speaker?			
Do you allow pauses and silence in your interactions?			
Do you acknowledge the speaker using affirmative language (e.g., Yes.... True...)?			
Do you paraphrase?			
Do you use probing strategies to allow the speaker to develop their message?			
Do you support elaboration that allows for clarification?			
Are you able to see another's point of view?			
Do you acknowledge other's ideas?			
Can you accept constructive criticism?			
Additional comments about your communication skills:			

Source: Adapted from Hentz S. (2010) by permission.

Tool 1.1

teaming. This tool provides a profile of key areas in communication as it relates to working in a team. Completing this activity individually and then sharing the results can contribute to greater awareness and cohesion within the team. This tool can also be used with students and for peer support and evaluation.

Effective communication is the foundation for relationship development based on the principles of trust and respect. Trust and respect may develop naturally, but in the context of collaborative working may require nurturing.

Trust

Trust is a positive, enabling, reciprocal, and powerful phenomenon. It is accompanied by feelings of comfort, confidence, and commitment, and actions of responsibility and protection. People trust each other with their perceptions, beliefs, or action about various topics. Trust and mistrust both act as a safety mechanism in our daily lives; therefore, the level of trust influences how active one participates within a group. Previous personal experiences can influence the ability to trust and often impacts present day responses. It is important to learn about each team member to gain an understanding of experiences that may impact the ability to trust.

Respect

Respect is synonymous with feelings of self-worth and well-being. Dillon (2007) identified the important role of respect in professional lives: "We may learn that jobs and relationships become unbearable if we receive no respect in them" (p. 1). Collaboration is built on mutual respect. One can disagree with another's opinions but must respect and appreciate the differing views or perspectives. In other words, participants must be able to agree to disagree on one level but come to a consensus about practice on another level. The following activity focuses on the definition of respect and promotes the growth of mutual respect between parents, students, and professionals.

Activity

In small groups of 3–6 people, ask participants in a circle formation to talk briefly about the definition of respect and how they know when they have someone's respect. Sharing examples helps to make the abstract phenomenon of respect more concrete for individuals and helps solidify a common definition/understanding for the group.

What Can We Do to Build and Maintain Trust and Respect?

Investment in developing trust at both individual and group levels reaps long-term rewards, both personally and professionally. The personal exchange of getting to know one another through trust-building activities involving emotional and physical participation offers a strong foundation for establishing trust. During the initial group meeting, structures, rules, guidelines, customs, and working practices need to be discussed to create higher levels of trust. Many readers may recall trust-building activities involving a blindfold or falling backwards into someone's arms. This type of trust-building exercise can be used in classrooms, workshops, and training seminars. However, the group dynamics and context will determine the pace and intensity of the trust-building activities to be used in team-building endeavors

Activities for Building Group Trust

Group activities require an appreciation of another's point of view with the development of mutual reliance through patience and communication. It is imperative to be sensitive to the responses of all participants and to choose activities based on the comfort levels of individuals within the group. The following are some activities for trust building at the group level.

- **Willow Branch**: A group forms two lines facing each other. A long, thin stick (tree branch, walking stick etc.) is placed across the group's index fingers. The goal of the group is to lower the rod to the ground without letting it fall. The rod is lifted and requires group concentration and effort to lower it to the ground successfully.
- **Balloon Fun**: A group forms a circle and a balloon is thrown into the center. The challenge is to keep the balloon off the floor but for each person to touch it alternating turns between group members.
- **Group Creative Storytelling**: A group creates a unified story from a set of sequential pictures that are randomly distributed. Each person describes the picture to others without revealing the picture. Members of the group then sequence themselves in relation to where the description of the picture fits into the story. The group shares the whole story.
- **Labyrinth**: Members of the group hold hands to form a long line. The appointed leader leads the group in, out, over, and above participants' joined hands to form a "labyrinth." The group's challenge is to unravel themselves without the chain of hands being broken.

Activities for Building Partner Trust

Partner trust-building activities are more personal than group activities and require a strong level of shared reliance and communication between individuals. The activities below illustrate joint activities for building effective partnerships.

- **Communication Charades**: In pairs each member is assigned the letter A or B. Partner A is designated as the "communicator" and B the "listener." Partner A has to communicate to partner B nonverbal information (a recent trip, a special time in his or her life) See **Tool 2.2, Reflection of Personal Stories** on page 23 for additional topics. Partner B has to listen and is able to ask open-ended questions, not questions that elicit "yes/no" answers. Partner A is told not to use words, sign language, or any other form of written communication. After a few minutes the partners swap roles. Afterward they debrief on the outcome and the process of the communication.
- **Following On**: One partner takes on the role of teacher and the other one the role of the student. The student may be blindfolded. It is the teacher's task to talk the student through an activity. Some examples of such activities are building a five-block tower, drawing shapes, or completing a puzzle. Partners swap roles and talk about strategies that were used to assist the student in the activity. A great resource that presents a range of such activities is www.wilderdom.com/games/initiativegames.html.

Incidents may happen that lead to diminishing trust, which will warrant sensitivity and openness in communication. A return to the continued application of effective communication strategies may help in this endeavor. This return may take the form of a reflective discussion where the partnership jointly decides on a course of action for the future. In addition, the conflict resolution activities presented in Chapter 2 may also be beneficial in rebuilding trust.

Roles and Responsibilities Across Collaborative Partnerships

People play many roles in their complex daily lives, such as parent, child, sibling, friend, enemy, confidante, among others. Individuals weave in and out of these roles when interacting and working with others. When working in a group, it is helpful to identify a facilitator to support clarification of roles and responsibilities and to continually evaluate group work. A collaborative facilitator may be the curriculum specialist, data coach, special educator, general educator, team leader, or an administrator. This responsibility can be rotated among members to allow, over time, an appreciation of how the roles affect the working of the team. Some of the roles involved in a collaborative partnership are recipient, equal partner, expert consultant, mentor, and coach.

- **Recipient:** In the role of the recipient, it is important to be open to the ideas of others, to allow time to process information, and to apply this information to professional practice. There are ways to receive information through mentoring and coaching that influence the success of the collaboration. For example, asking positive and constructive questions allows for clarification and understanding of the meaning of the communication.
- **Expert Consultant:** An expert consultant has valuable knowledge and expertise. It is important for the consultant to be sensitive to the setting, to have knowledge of the participants, and to apply expertise based on the need or area of concern.
- **Equal Partner:** At times, the role of equal partner is adopted with a colleague or a group of colleagues, such as shared teaching partnerships. This impacts the distribution of power within the context of a particular collaborative endeavor. In this framework, attention should be paid to the balance of activity, intellectual contribution, and effort of all partners to ensure that equal does indeed mean equal.
- **Mentor:** The role of mentor tends to focus upon, but is not limited to, a one-to-one relationship. The mentor has content expertise but also an understanding of how knowledge is translated into practice. A mentor supports such practical application based on the individual's responses to the new information and knowledge. A mentoring relationship, like all relationships in collaborative working, is reciprocal. Mentors also receive understandings, perceptions, and skills that can improve their personal and professional lives.
- **Coach:** To coach someone involves the actual modeling of desired behavior. A coach is able to demonstrate the practical "action" element of any new theoretical understandings. One can naturally be a mentor and a coach at the same time. In being a coach however, there is a level of expertise and experience in practice, accompanied by an ability to teach and demonstrate. For a free analysis of your personal and group strengths in the area of coaching and mentoring visit **www.franklincoveycoaching.com/free_assessment.**

There is a natural distribution of responsibility and authority in the administrative nature inherent in these roles. For example, an equal partnership requires equal distribution (or redistribution) of responsibility. This may involve the delegation of a task. This process of relinquishing this power can be challenging. Chapter 3 explores strategies for delegation in collaborative working. Knowing the working style of team members and appreciating their strengths and areas needing development will improve how new information is received and applied.

The Reflective Practitioner

Self-reflection, as it pertains to beliefs and understandings of the practice of working in a partnership, is an essential element of being a collaborative practitioner. Self-reflection can occur in the context of individual, partner, and group work. **Tool 1.2, All About Me** (p. 13), offers a structure for appreciating similarities and differences in personal thought processes. This tool can be shared orally or in a written format. Time must be provided for discussion of the responses.

In completing and sharing this tool, collaborators will be able to develop an appreciation for the perspectives and practices of their partners and will also allow for more sensitive and positive interactions. **Tool 2.1, Personal Leadership Qualities**, and **Tool 2.2, Reflection of Personal Stories** (in Chapter 2) can also be used to facilitate individual and partner reflection.

Group participants should be clear about the intention of the project by defining the project to ensure shared ownership. The group or team is encouraged to monitor and critique the process and outcomes of working together in order to improve teaching and learning. **Tool 1.3, Plan for Group Reflection** (p. 14), offers questions that can be completed on an individual or group basis to support a structured group reflection of the collaboration.

Using the information generated through this tool, team members will understand the process and outcome of the team efforts. This will have a positive effect on individual comfort levels, confidence, and the subsequent performance of the group.

Administrative Support for Collaborative Practice

Collaborative practice needs to operate in a system with the explicit support of leadership and administration. Some educators work tirelessly in "islands of collaboration" where there is little or no administrative appreciation and support. Many times collaboration flourishes despite administrative forces that may work to stifle collaborative efforts. To move toward greater levels of administrative investment and support, educators must communicate:

- information about the process of the collaboration.
- collaborative efforts that fit into strategic goals.
- efficient use of available resources. This may be about working smarter, not harder.
- evaluating the collaborative effort at key points as the year progresses.

When shared, collaboration may encourage similar projects across the school and provides documentation of the team's desire to increase administrative investment.

All About Me

Dialog Starters

Name:

Directions: Complete each open-ended statement. Share with your collaborative team members.

1. I respond well to...
2. The best way to motivate me is...
3. One thing you should know about me is...
4. I become defensive when...
5. The best quality I bring to a partnership is...
6. The quality I admire most in a professional partner is...
7. I am open to other ideas when...
8. The most important component of a working relationship is...
9. When I am not working, I like to...
10. I spend weekends...

Tool 1.2

Plan for Group Reflection

Team Members:

Directions: As a member of a collaborative partnership, complete the questions below. Identify three responses per question.

What are three possible strategies to increase our knowledge of the process and/or outcome?
How will additional information improve and contribute to the project?
What do we want to know about the process and/or outcome?
How will new information be shared and applied?
How will data be interpreted?

Tool 1.3

The Inter-relationship between Consultation, Collaboration and Co-Teaching

Consultation, collaboration, and co-teaching do not exist as separate entities; rather they are on a continuum of collaborative practice. A natural overlap exists among the practices that will vary within different collaborative partnerships. It is not necessary to keep them separate; indeed, viewing them as a continuum helps others appreciate the complex nature of an evolving partnership. Movement along the continuum depends on the nature of relationships, expertise, and context.

Definitions of Consultation, Collaboration, and Co-Teaching

A shared definition of the styles of professional partnerships provides an understanding of skills essential to team or group projects. The ultimate effectiveness of the tools and strategies presented in each of the subsequent chapters rely on an understanding of these key components.

- **Collaboration:** To collaborate is to work together in a joint intellectual and professional effort. This practice itself is not new, but it is gaining attention in the current drive for appropriate and effective environments for all learners. Collaboration takes place between two or more people and began, in some form, to become a school practice in 1975 with the passing of Public Law 94-142, the Education of All Handicapped Children Act, known as the Individuals with Disabilities Education Improvement Act, which opened classroom doors for students with disabilities. This practice, however, has been used in the corporate world for many years. Collaborative inclusive practices encompass an umbrella of skills ranging from consultation to co-teaching partnerships. Howard (2009) states that knowledgeable collaboration can provide teachers with a wide repertoire of rich strategies that make room for instructional choices and options according to the needs of each child.
- **Consultation:** Newman (2007) defines consultation as seeking advice and information from colleagues. In education, this translates into many different scenarios and involves the roles of consultant, mentor, and coach. Consultation can take the form of one meeting or ongoing meetings that evolve over time. For example, a parent of students with disabilities can be a consultative partner providing knowledge and expertise about the child that can be the foundation for instructional planning and team building. A teacher may consult with parents and other professionals both inside and outside the school context. The teacher receives support developing strategies and implements them in the classroom. Another example of consultation is an expert consultant implementing a highly focused project to create solutions for specific issues or concerns raised by administrators. District administrators subsequently make decisions based on the recommendations of the expert consultant.

There is a range of consultative practices involved in the continuum of collaboration. Defining elements of each of these practices are related to the amount of "action" that each member of the team contributes to the endeavor. Different team members have more active roles as they move along the continuum of collaborative practice. For example, an occupational therapist, following a collaborative planning session with the general education teacher, may come into class and model a range of Brain Gym activities. The occupational therapist would model these activities in the classroom for a specific time, and then the teacher takes over the activities, as she or he internalizes and applies the strategy; the occupational therapist then steps away. The therapist remains available for evaluation, support, and further consultation.

- **Co-Teaching:** Co-teaching is the ultimate collaborative teaching practice. An evolution of co-teaching is shared teaching based on parity—shared instruction, shared planning and shared evaluation. Teachers can co-teach for one class, for a series of classes, or for the whole day. In co-teaching, two educators accept *shared responsibility* for instructing *all* students in the classroom. There are a variety of co-teaching approaches: one teach and one observe, station teaching, parallel teaching, alternative teaching, teaming, and one teach and one assist. Each of these approaches are explored in Chapter 5. The practice of co-teaching has been inextricably linked to inclusive teaching that aids in meeting the demands for highly qualified teacher status. This method promotes partnerships among disciplines that capitalize on the strengths of different professionals.

Summary

When teams of people come together to work collaboratively, the complexity of an organization can be recognized and celebrated. Legislation embraces the concept of access to the general education curriculum for all students with disabilities and placement with peers to the maximum extent appropriate. This influences the nature of relationships among special and general educators and professionals within schools. Effective communication is the key to improving collaborative practice, which provides increased opportunities for success for students and teachers. The principles of trust, respect, and reflection affect the process of consultation, collaboration, and co-teaching. Embedded in the range of collaborative practices are the contributions of each participant and the recognition of their understanding, skills, and experiences. We need to be persistent in our support of collaborative partnerships to improve teaching and learning in an era of increased accountability in increasingly diverse and inclusive classrooms. A collaborative partnership is made up of people in a team, and it is well worth spending time improving how a team works together.

CHAPTER TWO

"Real teams don't emerge unless individuals on them take risks involving conflict, trust, interdependence and hard work."

Katzenbach & Smith

Teamwork

Teamwork is a collaborative effort by a group of people. In education, teams work to improve outcomes for students and educators. Understanding the personal qualities and experiences of each team member will positively influence the effectiveness of the team. The challenge of teamwork is to maximize the roles and responsibilities of each member and determine models of working together in fulfilling the team's mission. Sharing a positive vision with effective communication and passion for individual and group improvement is fundamental for the development of a successful team. Within this context, team members must adapt flexibility in thinking and be willing to improve personal skills and attributes.

Personal Skills and Attributes

There is no "I" in *team* but there is in *win*. An individual's personal skills and attributes is significant because this contribution to the team impacts the ultimate quality of the teamwork. For some people, the most difficult part of this process is the self-evaluation of personal skills, qualities, and experiences. To alleviate stress during the process, educators can structure evaluations as part of an informal event where the team breaks bread by sharing a snack, where the tone of acceptance is set by the facilitator, manager, or team leader.

It is beneficial to reflect on communication skills, personal qualities, and experiences. Integral to all processes are effective communication skills, which should be the initial focus of attention while building teaming skills. **Tool 1.1, Communication Checklist** in Chapter 1, can help identify an individual's current communication skills, strengths, and areas that need development. The components of communication however, can be ever-changing as individuals improve and increase communication skills.

Teacher as Leader

Gudwin and Salazar-Wallace (2010) found that teacher leaders exhibit some of the personal leadership qualities listed on **Tool 2.1, Personal Leadership Qualities**. Think about some of the leaders who have impacted you in a positive way. What characteristics did they possess? Think about your own attributes. Highlight the traits in Tool 2.1 that you see in yourself. Use the results of the survey to create an action plan to increase your leadership qualities. Sharing the results of the survey will help the team to allocate roles for a particular team initiative. It can also support team building and potentially influence future role assignment for different projects.

Team Member Roles

Several critical characteristics of effective teams enable individuals to develop an appreciation of diverse preferences, expertise, and experiences. Individuals also need to adopt different roles in the team. These roles are often dependant on the nature of the collaborative and the qualities of each member. The roles of each team member may change in relation to the context and expected outcomes. This illustrates the complexity of the interrelationships among the roles. According to Gudwin and Salazar-Wallace (2010), a coach or mentor often wears many hats, sometimes even simultaneously:

- The role of a **guide**: leading, guiding.
- The role of a **role model**: modeling lessons, acting as a role model in specific situations.
- The role of a **listener**: listening, not always providing advice, but real listening.
- The role of a **friend**: supporting as a trusted friend would.
- The role of a **counselor**: providing a shoulder to cry on, a hug, offering a dialogue of options.
- The role of a **family member**: offering a nurturing and trusting relationship.
- The role of a **lifeline**: being accessible and approachable, sharing knowledge.

Personal Leadership Qualities

Name: ______________________________

Directions: Think about your personal attributes. Highlight the qualities that you see in yourself. Put a star next to the qualities that you would like to add to your list of qualities.

A desire or interest in leadership	Open communication
The ability to influence others	Clout in the culture of the school
An ability to volunteer, be a "do-er"	A person who goes the extra mile
The ability to see the vision and help carry it out	A catalyst for change, even embracing change
A willingness to continue to learn and share	The ability to speak and others listen
Sometimes a quiet backstage worker that can get the job done	Part of a core group, the worker bees who are known to get the job done
A constant desire to improve teaching practices	Compassionate, competent, credible, and approachable

Personal Qualities Action Plan:

- ➢
- ➢
- ➢
- ➢

Source: Adapted From Gudwin, D. M. & Salazar-Wallace, M. D. (2010) by permission.

Tool 2.1

- The role of a **coach**: offering motivation, instructional coaching, a pep talk when needed.
- The role of an **advisor**: providing advice and feedback.
- The role of a **resource**: sharing resources such as professional books, websites, blogs, and teacher products.
- The role of a **co-teacher**: acting as a colleague, an equal, a peer teacher.
- The role of an **advocate**: supporting and sponsoring (p. 41).

What "hat" are you wearing right now? What role do you usually play? And finally, what additional role could you add to your toolbox?

By knowing our leadership qualities, focusing in on our roles, and practicing effective ways to communicate, we can successfully build and maintain valuable team relationships, which ultimately have a positive effect on our teaching and learning practices. From an investment perspective, it highlights the need to spend time nurturing each of the roles within the group to utilize individual strength and expertise.

Choosing Team Members

Developing an effective team begins with the individual. As with families, one may not have the opportunity to choose the members of a professional team. Therefore, initially there may be little identification with fellow team members because of the lack of knowledge of shared personal interests and content area. During time spent building relationships in the team, respect and empathy may develop, which results in a positive affect on the development of trust and friendships. Team-building strategies are used to nurture and develop trust and respect as illustrated in Chapter 1. These strategies can be applied to building relationships within the team structure.

Team members will feel more comfortable sharing personal information when expectations, customs, and ground rules are established. These norms should include the need to be nonjudgmental and the importance of confidentiality. Collaborative team members bring various experiences, ideas, and characteristics that add value to the synergy of the team. The more team members learn about each other, the greater the synergy. **Tool 2.2, Reflection of Personal Stories** (p. 23), is an exercise to help develop an understanding about perceptions regarding the affect of experiences, expectations, fears, and motivators of each team member. The responses can be shared in written or oral format.

Other formal and standardized tools are widely used to assess individual learning and thinking styles, which can offer insight into team participation. Each of these tools identifies information about the personal preferences that influence one's behavior. Many of these tools

Reflection of Personal Stories

Name: ________________________________

Directions: Select two or three prompts and write about your experiences.

- Share a great success story
- Write a short autobiography about events of your life
- Identify positive traits, talents, and strengths
- Share your hopes-both professionally and personally
- List achievements to date, including personal and professional accomplishments that go back to childhood
- Identify a challenging time in your life and how you overcame the challenge
- Provide examples of how you have made or make a difference in the lives of others
- Write about your mentor(s) and their contributions to your life
- Write about the happiest events of your life

Tool 2.2

have their roots in the early work of psychologists of the 1970s and 1980s, but remain pertinent in the exploration of personal styles and preferences in team effectiveness. Gregorc (1982), as discussed in James and Blank (2006), developed a tool that examines thinking styles and plots the results on the continuums of concrete to abstract and random to sequential thinking. The Myers-Briggs Type of Indicator (Quenk, 2000) offers an established and standardized assessment of personality types that allows insight into whether one is sensing, intuitive, judging, or perceptive in interactions with others. Both tools reflect interest in learning about styles and preferences, and their effect on personal and professional interactions. People who succeed and flourish are willing to adapt and grow by being truthful in their evaluations and personal reflections. In all of the tools discussed, there are no right or wrong answers or preferences, but the value lies in the development and awareness of individual strengths and contributions to the team.

Working in a Team

Teaching, student learning, and accountability are complex endeavors, and working with others in a team can positively affect success for teachers and students (Friend & Cook, 2009). It is important to be aware that some people have highly developed skills working independently, but may have areas of need when working in a team. Hentz (2010) identifies the characteristics of a successful team member: a high level of competence in the areas of conferencing, positive communication skills, collaborative problem solving abilities, embracing change, soliciting input from others, identifying instructional strategies and interventions, and maintaining relationships. **Tool 2.3, Collaborative Roles and Responsibilities** (p. 25), identifies members with particular strengths in areas of effective collaborative practice. Remember that more than one person may be assigned a particular role and that these roles can change over time and context.

Effective Teams

All forms of collaborative practice require a level of teamwork. Therefore, the challenge is to develop the skills and tools required to enter, participate, and maintain relationships in a team for the benefit of the students, staff, and school. Characteristics of an effective team are sharing common goals, operating in a respectful way, and demonstrating high levels of individual and group communication skills (Covey, 2004). Team effectiveness improves with constant reflection and evaluation of the operation of the team. **Tool 2.4, Team Effectiveness** (pp. 26–27), is a survey to assess the current level of a team in these important areas.

Each team member completes the survey independently and the results become prompts for group reflection, discussion, and evaluation. After this process, the team develops a plan of action for continued self improvement and team improvement.

Collaborative Roles and Responsibilities

Directions: Write down the name(s) of team members whose strengths contribute to the roles and responsibilities listed on the chart.

Collaborative Roles & Responsibilities	Names of Group Member(s)
Planning meeting agenda	
Meeting facilitator	
Provide personal and agreeable environment	
Soliciting input from all team members	
Summarizing the information	
Providing instructional strategies, resources, and interventions	
Time management of meeting	
Evaluating the collaborative	
Follow up on responsibilities of members	
Additional Roles and Responsibilities:	

Tool 2.3

Team Effectiveness

Name:

Directions: Read each prompt and assess your perceptions about the team. Place a check mark in the appropriate column. N = Never S = Sometimes A = Always

Our Team:	N	S	A
works together to establish goals.			
meets regularly with an agenda.			
starts meetings on time and keeps to scheduled time limits.			
ensures that all members are competent and used optimally.			
has an open line of communication.			
recognizes strengths and weaknesses of each member.			
has expectations regarding work performance.			
shares the role of facilitator (regular or rotating) who effectively keeps the discussion on track.			
participates in problem-solving and decision-making activities.			
clarifies for understanding of issues/ideas.			
Identifies action items and responsible individuals.			
agrees to disagree at times.			
provides tools and resources needed to perform.			

Tool 2.4

Our Team:	N	S	A
demonstrates respect through facial expression, body posture, and tone of voice.			
balances team member workload.			
compromises to reach agreement on the next steps.			
shares decision-making credit and blame (use "We" and "Us" vs. "I' and "You").			
allows conflict to arise then deals with it effectively and collaboratively.			
reinforces team members efforts to improve the process.			
regularly celebrates milestones and successes.			
has fun!			
Additional comments about our team effectiveness:			

Tool 2.4

Consultative Teams

Consultative teams can be comprised of people from a specific grade, school or district level, or a combination of all. Figure 2.1 illustrates some of the consultative teams that may be working in a school or district. This is not an exhaustive list, but it demonstrates the range of possible consultative groups.

Figure 2.1 Possible Consultative Groups

Student Support Team (SST) **Child Study Team (CST)** **Teacher Assistance Team (TAT)**	Professionals that form a problem solving group where an educator can refer a student of concern. A student must go to the SST or CST prior to referral for additional services.
English Language Learner (ELL)	Professionals meet to focus on issues affecting students who are culturally and linguistically diverse. The team meets regularly and includes diverse representation across areas of professional expertise.
Professional Learning Community (PLC)	A collegial group of school staff who are united in their commitment to student learning.
Districtwide Assistance Team	A group of districtwide personnel who are brought together for a particular focus (assessment, instruction, behavior, school performance). The districtwide assistance team can work with any number of schools at one time.
Response to Intervention (RTI) Team	A collaborative problem-solving team that utilizes data-driven dialogue to determine needs of individual students, research-based interventions, and ongoing progress monitoring. NOTE: It is imperative that all staff members have a clear understanding of the what and why of RTI.

Models of Working as a Team

In a team, there are various approaches when working with an individual or in a group. The Collaborative Problem-Solving Model is the practical application of working together in a joint intellectual and professional effort toward a common goal. An example is provided to increase awareness through our practical application.

Collaborative Problem-Solving Model

A collaborative problem-solving model can be used to generate possible solutions to an identified problem or concern. The problem-solving model is a facilitated process based on participant members being respectful, nonjudgmental, and solution driven. It is a four-step or tiered approach.

Step 1: Problem Identification: In this first step, the team defines the problem. What is the problem? To identify a problem, you need to review data on the expected level of performance. Is there a discrepancy between current and expected performance? Be sure to come to consensus about the problem.

Step 2: Problem Analysis: An analysis is initiated to look at the instruction, curriculum, environment, and learner to develop a hypotheses about possible causes for the identified problem. Why is this occurring? The team discusses issues and concerns related to the problem.

Step 3: Plan Development/Implementation: Members of the team propose possible solutions to achieve the desired outcome. Match the instructional strategy to the problem. What will be done to resolve the problem? This brainstorming activity provides a forum for the generation of creative solutions. Potential solutions are analyzed, along with the implications of managing and applying them in practical contexts. The team determines the best solution for the specific problem, one that seems feasible to all participants and in the contexts of the problem and desired outcomes. The individual or team proposing the problem develops the action plan, plans the steps, and determines data collection related to evaluation.

Step 4: Plan Evaluation: Did it work? The team reviews and analyzes the data. The team will then determine intervention decisions based on the review and analysis of data. The discussion will also include the progress and outcomes.

Tool 2.5, Collaborative Problem-Solving Plan (p. 30), offers a quick guide for the problem-solving process and a structure for teams to utilize to complete each step of the model. This offers a systematic process that a team can adapt to generate solutions to practical classroom issues. Students can also use it as a process to actively problem solve.

Collaborative Problem-Solving Plan

Teacher Name: ______________________________

Student Name: ______________________________

Date: ______________________Grade: ________

Participants:

1. **Problem Identification:** What is the problem?

2. **Problem Analysis:** Why is this occurring? (Examine Instruction, Curriculum, Environment, and Learner)

   Level of performance before intervention (baseline):

   Goal of Intervention: (Expected level of student performance)

3. **Plan Development:** What are we going to do about it? (Examine research-based interventions and match to student need)

   Plan Implementation: (Materials/Where/When)

   Person(s) Responsible:

4. **Plan Evaluation:** Did it work? How did the student respond to the intervention? Progress Monitoring (A graphic representation of progress)

   How and when will data be collected?

   Person(s) Responsible:

   Next Meeting Date:

Source: Reprinted with permission. Hentz (2009). *Response To Intervention: Practical Strategies and Tools for Implementation*

Tool 2.5

Example of Problem Solving in Practice

Participants: General Education Teacher, Special Education Teacher, Speech and Language Therapist

1. **Problem Identification:** Attending and participating in lead lesson for Writers Workshop. Robert (5th grade) appears off task during this time. He plays with objects in desk, talks with other children, and taps on the desk. He is unable to respond to teacher-directed questions, and when he moves on to independent workshop activities he continually asks questions about what he should be doing. Data collected demonstrates that Robert is engaged in off-task behavior 60% of the time and is unable to answer content questions.

2. **Problem Analysis:** Robert is included in the general education classroom with support from a speech and language pathologist. The general education teacher has tried suggested interventions to improve Robert's listening skills while in a large group lesson. Robert sits in the middle of the room with a friend who appears to encourage his off-task behavior. Robert is self-conscious and gets easily embarrassed in front of peers. Therefore, a more subtle intervention is required. Robert becomes defensive when asked to stop fiddling and can become uncooperative. When the class moves in to the workshop part of the lesson, Robert wanders and needs adult support to engage in an activity.

3. **Plan Development:** Possible interventions—preferential seating, visual aids to support comprehension, hand fidgets, pre-teaching vocabulary and concepts in speech therapy prior to lesson, nonverbal cues, positive reinforcement. Give Robert a visual aid of Writers Workshop tasks. Preteach concepts and vocabulary in speech therapy prior to lesson.

   Goal: Robert will attend to intro mini lesson for 15 minutes, correctly respond to 3 content questions posed by teacher, and begin independent activity on his own. The speech and language therapist will begin preteaching immediately. The general education teacher will use preferential seating, nonverbal cues, and visual aids.

4. **Plan Evaluation:** Robert will attend to the mini lesson for 15 minutes—teacher observation data. Robert will correctly respond to 3 content questions posed by teacher—response to question data collected by teacher. Robert will begin independent activity—teacher observation data. Team will meet to review data in 2 weeks.

This process has helped to maintain Robert in an inclusive context in school while improving his comprehension and on-task behavior.

Conflict Management

Conflict is a disagreement about ideas, principles, and people. Conflict is a sign that the psyche is trying to survive, to get its needs met, and to become whole again. In any group whose intent is to give every member a voice, there will be conflict. With appropriate techniques for understanding and managing the conflict, the relationships within the team will be strengthened. As with individual teaching and learning styles/preferences, there are many formal and standardized assessments on personal conflict management profiles.

Kenneth and Kilmann's (1999) work on conflict management has generated inventories based on the competing, collaborating, compromising, avoiding, and accommodating styles of conflict management. A *competing* style sees conflict as competition, and "winning" is so important that sometimes relationships may suffer. A *collaborating* style sees conflict as an opportunity to build relationships in the group while still being able to assert one's own position. A *compromising* style sees conflict as an opportunity to find the "common" ground between members who often give up their own position in order for facilitation to occur. An *avoidance* style often withdraws in the face of conflict and may give the impression that all is well to avoid conflict. An *accommodating* style sees relationships as more important than conflict and will often avoid conflict to maintain harmony. **Tool 2.6, Conflict Management Strategies** (p. 33), can be used to help identify one's preferred style.

The team can work together to reflect upon implications and solutions to a group profile of conflict management styles. All conflict management styles can benefit from the following strategies for managing conflict:

- remain calm
- look at the speaker
- don't interrupt the speaker
- don't adopt a defensive posture
- listen to what is said
- accept criticism of ideas without being defensive
- criticize ideas and not people
- don't talk about others behind their backs
- check the accuracy of the message (don't assume)
- validate the other person's feelings
- reflect on the other person's point of view
- use a tone of voice that emulates calmness
- avoid tones that suggest impatience, disgust, or sarcasm
- speak clearly and slowly at a moderate volume

Conflict Management Strategies

Name:

Directions: Review the following conflict management styles and their attributes. First, highlight your attributes when dealing with conflict and then select the style in the left column where you have highlighted the most attributes.

Conflict Management Style	Attributes
	When dealing with conflict, I...
Competing	▪ Stand up for my rights ▪ Am often assertive ▪ Defend my position ▪ Use influence appropriate to win my position ▪ Make efforts to see that I don't lose
Collaborating	▪ Work with others to solve problems ▪ Understand underlying concerns of others ▪ Learn from the insight of others ▪ Search for creative solutions ▪ State my needs and cooperate with others
Compromising	▪ Find the most expedient, acceptable solution ▪ Seek partial satisfaction for all parties ▪ Try to understand others' viewpoints ▪ Exchange concessions with others ▪ Am okay with partially satisfying all parties
Avoiding	▪ Postpone the issue until another time ▪ Softly sidestep the issue ▪ Steer clear of others when feeling threatened ▪ Avoid taking sides with others ▪ Try not to think about the conflict
Accommodating	▪ Try to satisfy others ▪ Sometimes neglect my own needs for the sake of others ▪ Avoid competing with others ▪ Try to be generous and giving ▪ Yield to the views of other

Source: Reprinted with permission from Barnitt (2006). Retrieved from www.cub.wsu.edu/Lead/library/resources

Tool 2.6

- attempt to reach agreement on a goal
- plan to return to the issue with an agreed-on agenda

Team Maintenance Strategies

For a team to succeed, spending time reflecting on accomplishments and learning more about individuals will yield positive results. There are many approaches for acknowledging accomplishments resulting from collaborative efforts. These may include spontaneous and tangible rewards, public recognition, and private acknowledgement of team successes. Planning social activities and celebratory events can provide an informal forum for acknowledgement, discussion, and fun. These activities can assist in community building and contribute to a sense of belonging for each team member. Remember, a team that can play together can stay together.

Summary

Teaming in schools is a complex process. The choice of teamwork approaches has a major influence on the subsequent decisions and outcomes of that team. The personal attributes that are highlighted through the self-audits offer a way for teams to acknowledge the unique contributions of all participants. Strong communication skills and respectful relationships are vital to an effective team. School administrators, leaders, teachers and professionals should make informed choices about team organization to increase the successful outcome of the team.

The collaborative problem-solving model offers a valuable way to generate solutions and create alternatives to a current situation. Creating a successful team is not a one-step process and involves the willingness of all stakeholders to continuously adapt and change. Teamwork among professionals and educators is key to providing meaningful and successful experiences for a diverse population of students, parents, and professionals. The practical application of teaming techniques will positively affect the shared practices of collaboration, consultation, and co-teaching.

CHAPTER THREE

"We will surely get to our destination if we join hands."

Aung San Sau Kyi (Burmese Political Leader)

Collaboration

Collaboration involves working with someone in a joint intellectual effort to find a solution to an identified issue or to create a joint development. Collaborative skills are at the heart of effective practices that are involved in consultation and co-teaching. "Collaboration is a process to reach goals that cannot be achieved acting singly (or, at a minimum, cannot be reached efficiently). As a process, collaboration is a means to an end, not an end in itself" (Bruner, 1991, p. 6). Collaborative work has become a mainstay of current education initiatives. Least restrictive environment, response to intervention, highly qualified status of teachers, inclusion, and class size legislation could all potentially benefit from collaborative work. Fostering collaboration and interconnectedness is important for classrooms, schools, and school districts to provide cohesive services that benefit the learner (Bassett, Campbell, Hirsch, Hupfeld, & Reichardt, 2004).

The level of responsibility each member of the team has in a collaborative partnership varies depending on individual qualities and his or her roles in relation to the planning, implementation, and evaluation of the initiative. This contribution of differing expertise affects the quality of work in classrooms, schools, and districts. The central goal of collaborative practice is the formation of a partnership that supports:

- improved communication between participants.
- fusing the strengths and expertise of each participant.
- improved student outcomes that are focused on student learning preferences, needs, and strengths.
- appraisal of the range of instructional strategies.
- appraisal of the environment.

Through collaborative practices, the performance of all students can improve.

Parents as Collaborative Partners

Educators have long recognized that parent involvement in education increases student achievement (Hentz, 2007). Effective parent-teacher communication and collaboration should be initiated as the school year begins. This can provide a forum for becoming acquainted as individuals and to allow the teacher to share information about student expectations, classroom rules, and teacher-parent communication methods. It is also a good time to gather information about the student's strengths, needs, and interests. There are many activities to enhance communication and collaboration that may include a classroom orientation or open house, parent-teacher conference, phone call, or written communication.

Qualities of a Collaborator

Some people are born collaborators while others need to develop skills to become an active member of a team. Collaborative team members do more than just work together. Each individual possesses qualities that add to the value of the relationship. Friend & Cook (2009), who have been instrumental in the development of effective school collaborative practices, suggest that collaboration should build upon voluntary participation, mutual respect and parity among participants, a shared sense of responsibility and accountability, and an equitable distribution of available resources. In reality, there may not be a choice to collaborate; the needs of students will demand it, and in these instances the collaboration with colleagues is imperative. There are key tools related to planning, implementation, and evaluation of collaborative work that make the process of collaboration more explicit. Sensitivity to the specific context will determine the application of each tool. Choosing which tool to apply demands sensitivity to the context both in which tool will be used and the composition of the team using the tool.

Tool 3.1, Qualities of a Collaborator (p. 40), is a self-evaluation audit of current qualities that support successful participation in collaborative practice. The survey identifies strengths and weaknesses of fundamental collaborative skills to increase awareness and support for each person in the partnership.

Surveys can be completed for each different partnership to reflect the varying levels of expertise and confidence with the specific content of the current venture. The more honest the response by individuals the more useful the generated information will be to build on the collaborative qualities of all participants. Time spent building the qualities of each individual will positively influence outcomes.

Roles and Responsibilities

A vital element of successful collaboration is the assignment or negotiation of clear of roles and responsibilities based on the qualities of each person. As the collaboration becomes more advanced, the roles and responsibilities will be ever-changing, with people taking on different roles depending on the setting and needs of students and educators. Members should discover other roles to fulfill as personal and professional qualities strengthen. Awareness of individually assigned responsibilities helps create a transparent and supportive context for planning, implementation, and evaluation stages of collaborative working.

Planning

Collaborative planning time has major potential, but can also be a challenge for the success of projects in schools and districts (Ahearn, 2005). Creating a long- or short-term time management plan can help make best use of limited time allocation. Barnitt (2006) offers planning suggestions.

- Persuade administration to create times in the schedule for shared planning.
- Utilize professional development days and trainings.
- Capitalize on resources to facilitate joint planning time. For example, use interns, student teachers, specialists, coaches, counselors, and administrators.
- Across a group, take turns covering for one another.
- For specific duties, arrange to be released or to cover each other.
- Write a grant and use the money to facilitate planning time.
- Be creative and flexible with time. For example, leave early on Monday afternoon to allow more sustained joint planning on Wednesday afternoon.
- Work with administrators to include a goal related to collaborative working within the strategic plan to allow for funding opportunities.

Qualities of a Collaborator

Name:

Direction: Rate your current qualities. N = Never S = Sometimes A = Always

Qualities	N	S	A
1. I am confident facilitating a meeting.			
2. I actively participate.			
3. I can listen to other perspectives.			
4. I verbally acknowledge other perspectives.			
5. I use nonverbal cues to demonstrate acknowledgement			
6. I am comfortable expressing my opinion.			
7. I am able to accept changes.			
8. I appreciate the different contributions of team members.			
9. I believe in my professional expertise.			
10. I know my strengths and accept the strengths of others.			
11. I have a positive attitude.			
12. I can summarize information.			
13. I perceive conflict as a learning opportunity.			
14. I continually search for improvement.			

Tool 3.1

Once an overall time management plan is established, "working smart" will get the most out of time spent planning together. **Tool 3.2, Collaborative Team Action Plan** (p. 42), offers a structure for the meeting that includes elements for moving from planning to implementation.

Frattura and Capper (2007) emphasize the strong effect of varied collaborative teams in improving and maintaining integrated comprehensive services across a school and district. They highlight the importance of linking collaborative partnerships to systems goals; something already discussed in relation to increasing administrative support. It is essential to be aware of, and respond to, the professional development needs of collaborative members. These needs can be related to the product or process of the initiative. **Tool 3.3, Professional Development Needs Assessment** (p. 43), illustrates professional development needs across the team. Members individually evaluate their current knowledge, application, and needs, which are also used to identify members that can contribute to the professional development of others in the group.

Implementation

A shared understanding of roles, responsibilities, goals, and outcomes is key to a succesful implementation. Practice can be across the continuum of consultation to co-teach models of working in teams. Clarity of different roles, responsibilities, and expectations will help to improve professional confidence, risk taking, and practice. Collaborative partnerships come together at different times and at varying levels to support student and teacher performance. While Chapters 4 and 5 discuss the practices of consultation and co-teaching, **Tool 3.4, Collaborative Activities and Responsibilities** (p. 44), illustrates the range of activities that could be implemented to ascertain the roles and responsibilities of individuals working in a team. The implementation stage of collaborative working should be fun, rewarding, and exciting.

This tool provides activities that bring professionals together to create new contexts for learning. Classroom environments developed from universal design for learning principles incorporate such innovation as a natural part of the classroom and learning community (Villa & Thousand, 2005). An integral part of the implementation stage is the ability to delegate effectively. Indeed, the biggest challenge is sharing responsibility for the completion of activities and tasks.

Collaborative Team Action Plan

Team members present: Date of meeting:
Focus of Meeting:
Actions emerging from meeting: 1. 2. 3. 4.
Responsibilities and time frame of completion of action: 1. 2. 3. 4.
Date and time of review meeting:

Tool 3.2

Professional Development Needs Assessment

Name: ______________________________

Directions: Reflect on your needs for professional development. Put an X in the box that illustrates your level of knowledge and application. Describe your preferred learning preference. If you are willing to be a trainer on a specific topic, place a check mark in the final column.

Topic	High Level of Need	Moderate Level of Need	Minimal Level of Need	Comments: Write a more specific description regarding your need.	Describe your preferred learning preference: on line, coaching, training workshop, etc.	Willingness to be a trainer
Classroom Management						
Differentiated Instruction						
Instructional Strategies						
Content Knowledge						
Literacy Centers						
Collaboration						
Co-Teaching						
Conflict Management						
Technology						
Data Management						
Data Analysis						
Other						

Tool 3.3

Collaborative Activities and Responsibilities

Directions: Review the collaborative activity and write down the name(s) of the person responsible for the task.

Activities	Person Responsible
Plan for content area	
Determine instructional strategies	
Create a study guide	
Write lecture notes on board or on handout	
Provide hands-on activities	
Preteach or reteach	
Provide individual instruction	
Adapt materials	
Develop alternative assignment	
Teach learning strategies	
Monitor class work completion	
Manage assistive technology	
Monitor IEP goals	
Develop literacy centers	
Adapt physical classroom environment	
Complete progress notes	
Read aloud tests	
Development of alternative assessment	
Record student grades	

Tool 3.4

Delegation is particularly pertinent to the success of partnerships, as it demonstrates relationships built upon value, trust, and respect. The success of delegation relies on participants being in agreement about the task and expected outcomes. When making decisions about delegation, a partnership should reach agreement on the six points listed below.

1. Define the scope of the activity.
2. Determine the degree of authority needed. Remember, authority is different from responsibility. Decide on ways of informing others of this delegated authority. Try to foresee any blocks to acceptance of the authority. Plan action to overcome these blocks.
3. Set a time schedule.
4. Define the results expected. Be specific.
5. Agree to and establish the process for measuring successful completion.
6. Inform the team about the general scope of the delegated task.

Tool 3.5, Audit of Effective Delegation of Responsibilities (p. 46), offers an indication of how prepared the partners are for delegation. These practices can be developed at an individual and group level to form the foundation for successful delegation.

This tool helps assess individual skill levels, the amount of responsibilities to be delegated and therefore influences the degree of delegation that takes place. It may be that this tool identifies areas for development that need to take place before full delegation.

Evaluation of Collaboration

It is important to evaluate the process of collaboration to ensure success and appropriate future goal setting. Lipman (1997) identifies potential advantages of evaluating the process of collaborative groups as:

1. Building dynamic rapport among team members.
2. Building the climate for streamlined communication.
3. Stimulating creativity.
4. Discovering innovative ways of strategizing and solving challenges.
5. Highlighting hidden problems and agendas.
6. Appreciating individual differences and strengths.
7. Learning to trust.
8. Welcoming and managing change.
9. Strengthening teamwork and motivation.
10. Learning and having fun at the same time.

Audit of Effective Delegation of Responsibilities

Directions: Read each statement and choose the frequency box that applies to your current delegation practices.

Rate your current qualities. N = Never S = Sometimes A = Always

Delegation Practice	N	S	A
Agreement on the delegated task			
Shared and agreement on performance standards			
Appropriate professional expertise for the delegated task			
Clear objectives			
Shared confidence in each other's capabilities			
A level of self-confidence			
Acceptance that others may perform better			
Shared responsibilities for tasks			
Understanding of the responsibility			
Follow-up procedures for the delegated task			
Balance team member workload			

Tool 3.5

Evaluating Collaboration

Name: ______________________________

Directions: Complete this evaluation individually and then share as a team. Take a few minutes to write notes on the following:

Describe how the collaborative team worked well.
Describe a positive contribution of each team member.
Describe how the collaborative teamwork affected outcome-based activities.
Describe one area you would like the team to work on to strengthen collaboration.
Identify any additional resources that would strengthen collaboration at your school (material or personnel).

Tool 3.6

Tool 3.6, Evaluating Collaboration (p. 47), supports an evaluation of work accomplished by the team. At this stage, the most important additional role is identifying a person to offer constructive critique for reflection.

Completion of this tool can inform future planning and management of the collaborative team, and can ensure that the perspectives of each member are valued. A team may have to negotiate future group decisions based on individual perspectives gathered here.

Summary

In collaborative teams, people work together to achieve a goal or to solve a problem. The qualities of each individual influence the success of any collaborative relationship. Nurturing an individual's ability to participate in teams can influence the process and outcomes of the collaborative venture. Tools related to planning, delegation, implementation, and evaluation illustrate the need for structured processes to aid reflection that will affect collaborative practices. Teams should take time to evaluate the workings of a collaborative group and the process of collaboration. This not only can influence outcomes, but also can help to create a way of working that seeks continual improvement. The time dedicated to the process and outcomes of collaboration delivers positive returns.

CHAPTER FOUR

"When a team of dedicated individuals makes a commitment to act as one ... the sky's the limit."

Unknown

Consultation

To consult is to share expertise through the exchange of professional and intellectual information. It is part of the development of an effective support structure and enables schools to meet the challenges of a diverse student population. Consultative partners will vary based on the needs of each individual. Through consultation, educators receive support to initiate change and to improve outcomes in the classroom, school, and districts. Key components of effective consultation are the contribution of professional expertise, the application of this expertise to the practical context, and the quality of the evaluative process.

Consultative Partnerships

One of the initial tasks in the consultation process is the identification of potential consultative partners. **Tool 4.1, Checklist of Potential Consultation Partners** (p. 52), provides a checklist of possible partners within the educational field. Consultation can occur one-on-one with individuals from the same team or school, the district, or an expert consultant. The determination of potential partners should be based on the current issue or need. This translates to varied models

Checklist of Potential Consultation Partners

Name:________________________________

Directions: Prioritize appropriate consultation partners by numbering in the order of choice.

_____Parents	_____Student
_____Grade level teacher(s)	_____Administrator
_____Special education teacher	_____Paraprofessional
_____Data coach	_____Other colleagues
_____Students' peers	_____ESOL teacher
_____Reading specialist	_____Occupational therapist
_____Speech and language therapist	_____Physical therapist
_____School guidance counselor	_____Educational psychologist
_____Behavior specialist	_____School nurse
_____Clinical psychologist	_____Medical doctor
_____Curriculum Leader	_____Media specialist
_____School social worker	_____District specialist
_____Assistive Technology Specialist	_____Outside consultant
_____Other potential consultation partners:	

Tool 4.1

of consultation practice: A teacher may consult with parents and other professionals from inside and outside the school context; a speech pathologist or doctor may consult with a specialist or another related service provider and a county or district may consult with an expert consultant. Consultation may be an ongoing process, which evolves over time. It is important to build an effective consultation team that is both realistic and manageable. This often involves prioritizing collaborative partners.

Parents as Consultative Partners

Consultation with parents to ascertain knowledge regarding their child should be ongoing. Developing an open communication system and providing opportunities for the parents to contribute can have a positive effect on student achievement. The parent can help teachers and other professionals to better understand the needs of the student and families. Keeping the parent involved and informed of all processes of consultation about their child can strengthen the parent-teacher relationship. When an issue or concern involves a child, educators must have the parent as part of the team for support.

Circles of Support

"Circles of Support," as shown in **Tool 4.2, Consultative and Collaborative Partners** (p. 54), comprise a mapping tool to identify key support personnel that may offer advice in a specific situation. These support circles will change and evolve with time, need and context. This strategy, developed from research and development in "Circles of Influence," recognizes the power of the individual response to issues of organizational development (Covey, 2004). In the school setting, support circles recognize the value of an individual's personal and professional experience in creating solutions for both the student and teacher. For example, a student-focused support circle developed by a teacher to evaluate consultation support for a student experiencing behavioral challenges, can include the parent, a behavioral specialist, and an instructional or curriculum specialist. A teacher-focused support circle may also be developed by a teacher to identify potential consultation support to aid the development of a particular instructional or behavioral strategy. The tool helps in the reflection on why a specific person or professional would be a valuable consultation partner. Such reflection is particularly important in an era of scarce resources.

Request for Support

Before the first consultation meeting, the completion of a "Request for Support" should be prepared to help identify the area of concern. It is entirely appropriate at this stage for the concern to be general in nature. **Tool 4.3, Request for Student Support** (p. 55), is a tool for completing this process, and is based on student need for support. Professionals and parents may utilize this request at any time to receive support for the student.

Consultative and Collaborative Partners: Circles of Support

Teacher: Date:

Student: Parent:

Directions: In the blank circles, identify potential consultative and collaborative partners and their possible contribution.

Student

General Education Teacher

Parent

Source: Reprinted from Hentz (2009) by permission.

Tool 4.2

Request for Student Support

Name:

Requested consultation partner(s):

Directions: Place a check mark in the area(s) of concern or need.

____ Tardiness
____ Attendance
____ Conduct
____ Failure to achieve outcomes
____ Decline in academic performance

____ Work skills
____ Study/organization skills
____ Reading skills
____ Math skills
____ Written expression skills

Additional comments: ____

____

____

____

____

____

Area of student strengths: ____

____

Actions already taken: ____

____

____

Consultation is scheduled for: ____

Tool 4.3

Teachers may also request advice and support in their personal repertoire of teaching practices. **Tool 4.4, Request for Teacher Support** (p. 57), is a tool to identify the area of need to support the teacher's teaching. Schools may have an educator on campus that could provide professional development or modeling for individual teachers needing support.

Consultation Needs Assessment

A more detailed student needs assessment is the next step of the consultation and ensures clarification of the issue or need. During the consultation meeting, **Tool 4.5, Student Assessment** (p. 58), provides a structure to identify the specific academic, behavioral, social, and environmental needs of the student. The focus of the consultation will change as the student assessment becomes more specific. An educator may also use **Tool 3.3, Professional Development Needs Assessment**, to make a more detailed determination of their area of need. Discussion of the data generated by these tools becomes the foundation for development of subsequent strategies and interventions.

Managing the information generated from the consult is an important part of the process and provides documentation for accountability. **Tool 4.6, Consultation Plan** (p. 59), is an example of an action and evaluation plan for measuring progress, which also identifies next steps. This becomes the focus of subsequent consultation, thus ensuring coherence and continuity of targeted advice over a longer period of time.

Consultation Logs

For students with an individualized education program (IEP), educators must keep a log of any consultation that occurs. This records progress for students needing consultation support and will ensure that the requirements of the IEP are met. In a consultation log, the nature of the data collected will depend on the complexity of student need. However, a consultation log is, by its very nature, a working document that requires continuous updating. Consultation may occur daily, weekly, monthly or quarterly depending on the needs of the individual student. **Tool 4.7, Consultation Log** (p. 60), illustrates a consultation log for documenting the process focused on a student with an IEP.

Evaluation of the Consultation

It is vital to monitor and evaluate both the process and outcome of the consultation continually. **Tool 4.8, Consultation Evaluation** (p. 61), offers a structure to share expectations and outcomes and documents the changing nature of the consultation. All participants should contribute to the evaluation to support shared ownership of the process and outcomes.

Request for Teacher Support

Name: ______________________________ Date:__________

Directions: Place a check mark in the area(s) needing assistance.

____ Communicating with others

____ Increasing class participation

____ Improving attendance

____ Motivating students to learn

____ Working with my paraprofessional or co-teacher

____ Using data to drive instruction

____ Managing behavior

____ Reading strategies

____ Writing strategies

____ Learning/Literacy centers

____ Differentiating instruction

____ Increasing awareness of students with diverse needs (ESOL, students with disabilities, at risk)

Additional comments: ____

____

____

____

Area of strength: ____

____

Actions taken: ____

Consultation scheduled: ____

Tool 4.4

Student Assessment

Strengths and Concerns

Student name: ___________________________ Grade: _______Date: ________

Completed by: ___________________ Relationship to student: ___________________

Directions: Please check relevant items and make comments.

1. <u>Academic Performance</u>

Strengths
- ___Goal oriented
- ___Motivated to achieve in school
- ___Completes classwork
- ___Asks for additional assistance
- ___Hands in all assignments
- ___Participates in class discussions
- ___Responds to individualized instruction
- ___Works well in cooperative groups
- ___Has skills to plan ahead

Concerns
- ___Frequently tardy
- ___Skips class
- ___Failing subject(s)
- ___Demonstrates inconsistent daily work
- ___Does not actively participate
- ___Difficulty with constructive criticism
- ___Work not handed in
- ___Not responding to strategies

2. <u>Interpersonal Relationships</u>

Strengths
- ___Understands rules and consequences
- ___Exhibits responsible behavior
- ___Accepts personal responsibility
- ___Resists negative peer pressure
- ___Optimistic about future
- ___Seeks to resolve conflicts
- ___Values friends
- ___Has positive peer interactions
- ___Enjoys helping others
- ___Works well in cooperative groups
- ___Involved in art or music
- ___Involved in sports and/or clubs

Concerns
- ___Redirection to task
- ___Defiance of authority
- ___Disrupts class
- ___Displays extreme negativism
- ___Not responsibiile for behavior
- ___Destructs school property
- ___Fights
- ___Uses obscene language and gestures
- ___Has inappropriate peer relationships
- ___Talks about alcohol/drug use
- ___Displays odd/inappropriate behaviors
- ___Mood swings
- ___Vandalizes property

3. <u>Family Issues:</u>

Strengths
- ___Positive family communication
- ___Parent is actively involved in school
- ___Parents support student to achieve

Concerns
- ___Poor communication with school
- ___Low parental involvement in the school
- ___Running away from home

4. <u>Community:</u>

Strategies
- ___Actively participates in community service
- ___Maintains employment

Community Risk Indicators
- ___ Vandalism (outside of school)
- ___ Possession of alcohol and drugs
- ___ Known arrests/convictions
- ___ Loss of interest in job performance
- ___ Frequent changes in school placement

Tool 4.5

Consultation Plan

Date:

Name of Participants:

Problem identification:

Suggested solutions/interventions:

Plan implementation/recommendation:

Evaluation and progress monitoring tool:

Person responsible:

Date of next meeting:

Tool 4.6

Consultation Log

Student name:	Teacher:
Consult with:	Date:
Concern:	
Recommendation:	
Additional comments:	

Student name:	Teacher:
Consult with:	Date:
Concern:	
Recommendation:	
Additional comments:	

Student name:	Teacher:
Consult with:	Date:
Concern:	
Recommendation:	
Additional comments:	

Tool 4.7

Consultation Evaluation

Directions: In your consultative team complete the evaluation statements.

Names and roles of consultation partners:

Focus of consultation:

Outcome of Consult

Goal of consult:

Agreed criteria for success:

Nature and detail of evaluative data collected:

Interpretations from evaluative data:

Process of Consult

Particular strengths/contributions of consultation partners:

Emerging problematic issues in the process of the consultation:

Potential solutions for the future:

Tool 4.8

In using this tool, consultation partners may or may not continue with the current focus, may change the focus, or may discontinue the consultation. This tool will also generate feedback for future consultations and provide important progress monitoring for all involved. For example, teachers may draw information from this to share with parents at a parent teacher meeting. Consultation can be complex and may lead to confusion. It is important to have a holistic view of the process. **Tool 4.9, Checklist of the Consultation Process** (p. 63), provides a quick overview of the different stages. This tool can be used throughout the consultation process, but remember that not every consultative initiative will need to complete everything every time.

Summary

Consultation partnerships can enrich and support work in classrooms, schools, and districts. The identification of consultative partners varies depending on need and context. Consultation with parents will yield positive effects on student outcome. Awareness of Support Circles, the identification of specific student and teacher needs, the process of evaluation, and monitoring progress are essential components of effective consultation. Educators can use practical tools and strategies to manage the process and outcomes in an effective and meaningful way. Consultation offers a valuable level of expert support for educators; who are, in turn, responsible for the translation of this to practice. The sharing of the responsibility and practice of teaching moves into the realm of co-teaching.

Checklist of the Consultation Process

Directions: List the names of all participants and record dates of completion of the tasks.

Names of participants:

Date ________________ Checklist of Potential Consultation Partners

Date ________________ Circles of Support

Date ________________ Request for Student/Teacher Support

Date ________________ Student Assessment

Date ________________ Consult Plan

Date ________________ Consultation Summary

Date ________________ Consultation Log

Date ________________ Consultation Evaluation

Date ________________ Professional Development Needs Assessment

Tool 4.9

"Real dialogue is when two or more people become willing to suspend their certainty in each other's presence."

David Bohm

Co-Teaching

Co-teaching is sharing the expertise of professionals to create a teaching and learning environment conducive to positive student outcomes and teacher success. On the continuum of collaborative practices, shared teaching is the most complex where practitioners work together and share their physical and intellectual space to create something neither could create on their own. The concept of co-teaching promotes active partnerships among disciplines to blend individual expertise. Co-teachers share expertise and instructional responsibility for a single group of students with mutual ownership and joint accountability. A general education teacher could co-teach the content-specific curriculum with the special educator. Co-teaching can create a dynamic learning environment and is a unique approach for teaching students.

Co-Teaching Partnerships

There are a variety of co-teaching partnerships between teachers and other professionals. The co-teaching partnerships that may exist are:

General Education Teacher with:

- general education teacher (grade/content)
- special education teacher
- speech and language pathologist
- occupational therapist
- physical therapist
- district specialist
- other related service professionals

Special Education Teacher with:

- general education teacher (grade/content)
- speech and language pathologist
- occupational therapist
- physical therapist
- district specialist
- special education teacher
- other related service professionals

Building a relationship together is essential for co-teachers to have the opportunity to explore and blend philosophies, strengths, and needs. Some educators voluntarily work in a co-teaching structure, bringing their personal and professional styles and skills to the approach. Sometimes, however, professionals are placed into a co-teaching partnership with minimal input or training, which can result in confusion, fear, and frustration. Administrators and educators considering this model need to understand the processes involved in co-teaching and the need for opportunities to develop a rapport between teaching partners. In an effective co-teaching classroom, a positive, collegial relationship between two educators is essential and often takes time and effort to develop (Gately, 2005). Teachers must have support and training to learn about their co-teaching partners and to discuss styles and expectations. The first step is to reflect on individual skills, learning styles, experiences, attributes, and expectations. The ultimate goal is for both professionals to be invested and engaged in the shared teaching.

Developing rapport and an understanding for each person's communication style and reflecting on the co-teaching model can be used as a springboard for discussion. Previous chapters have presented tools for personal and shared assessment to provide an understanding of individual teacher needs, preferences, strengths, and expectations which are effective in building the relationship between collaborative partners (Chapter 1—**Tool 1.1, Communication Checklist**; Chapter 2—**Tool 2.1, Personal Leadership Qualities, Tool 2.2, Refection of Personal Stories, Tool 2.3 Survey of Personal Qualities of Roles**; Chapter 3—**Tool 3.1, Qualities of a Collaborator**).

The next step requires a more in-depth analysis of expectations and skills that relate specifically to the co-teaching partnership. **Tool 5.1, Am I Ready to Co-Teach?**

(p. 68), can be used during the early stages of the co-teaching partnership to highlight personal similarities and differences. The survey can be independently completed and then shared with colleagues for discussion.

Feedback from this tool will offer points for discussion and negotiation in preparation for co-teaching. At the initial stages of the partnership, it is important to share these beliefs, understandings, and experiences about the concept and practice of co-teaching. The self-assessment survey, **Tool 5.2, Teacher Survey of Co-Teaching** (p. 69), is another example for gathering and sharing information about beliefs and reflections on previous experiences of co-teaching. Remember that everyone needs to have the same goal: to help children learn.

The dialogue generated from the survey can be the foundation for the decision making process for the co-teaching structure. The partnership evolves and strengthens with shared understandings of the concept of co-teaching.

Classroom Expectations

Sharing classroom expectations is an important element of a successful co-teaching partnership. Teachers need to be ready to communicate with each other about disciplinary matters, academic expectations, parental involvement, procedures, and co-teaching approaches. This proactive communication provides a structure to develop an awareness of individual and shared expectations. It is okay to agree to disagree about personal philosophies, but what is important is the acceptance of shared and consistent practices. **Tool 5.3, My Expectations in the Classroom** (pp. 70–71), can be a forum for a discussion about individual responses to all aspects of classroom practice.

Regardless of whether one is teaching in a preschool, elementary school, high school, or university, it is important to establish working relationships with other teachers. The goal of this tool is to communicate and negotiate a resolution of differences to achieve consensus about classroom practices. After completing and sharing **Tool 5.3, My Expectations in the Classroom**, the co-teachers will be ready to examine how roles and responsibilities will be allocated.

Roles and Responsibilities of Co-Teachers

One of the initial tasks for identifying roles and responsibilities is to develop a shared list of responsibilities deemed necessary in a particular co-teaching environment. Various responsibilities can be assigned, shared, and reassigned as the relationship and co-teaching practice develops. **Tool 5.4, Responsibilities of Co-Teachers** (p. 72), will have varied responsibilities depending on the skills, knowledge, and experience of team members based on the classroom, teacher and student needs. **Tool 5.4, Responsibilities of Co-Teachers** offers a structure to discuss responsibilities.

Am I Ready to Co-Teach?

Directions: Write your responses to assist in determining if you are ready for this relationship. After you have completed the survey, meet with your colleagues to share your responses by taking turns reading the responses. After you have read all of your responses, reflect on the reactions to the responses.

1. My attitude about teaching students with disabilities in a general education classroom is ...
2. What I can bring to the co-teaching partnership is ...
3. What I would like to develop through a co-teaching partnership is ...
4. Some things my co-teacher needs to know about my teaching and learning preferences (noise, organization, structure) are ...
5. My biggest challenge in thinking about co-teaching is ...
6. My communication strengths are ...
7. My areas of communication need are (e.g. managing conflict and disagreement) ...
8. To maintain feedback about co-taught lessons I am willing to ...
9. My preferred organization and structure for co-teaching is (daily, a few times per week, content focused, assessment focused) ...
10. The training I need before implementing co-teaching is ...

Please use the remainder of the space on this page to share any additional thoughts, ideas, or recommendations you have for working in a co-teaching partnership.

____

____

____

____

____

Source: Adapted from Hentz (2007) Teach Smart: Practical Strategies and Tools for Educators, VIEW Inc. by permission.

Tool 5.1

Teacher Survey of Co-Teaching

Dialog Starters

Name:______________________________ Grade Level______________

Directions: Respond to the following prompts.

1. How would you define co-teaching?

2. Discuss the various approaches of co-teaching.

3. Does co-teaching provide support for students experiencing academic or behavioral difficulties? Why or why not?

4. If you were a co-teacher, what type of support (time, strategies, planning, scheduling) would you need for implementation?

5. Do you have experience working in a co-teaching model? List successes and concerns about your experiences.

6. Describe the professional development you may require to participate in the co-teaching service delivery.

7. State three teacher benefits for the implementation of the co-teaching model.

8. State three student benefits for participating in a co-taught classroom.

9. Can all students receive an appropriate education with co-teachers in a general education classroom? Why or why not?

10. How can we ensure that both teachers are instructional leaders in the co-taught classroom?

Tool 5.2

My Expectations in the Classroom

Name:

Directions: Individually complete this worksheet by listing your expectations for the following topics. After completion, share the responses with your co-teacher and discuss your reactions to the responses.

I have the following expectations for my classroom:

1. Parent communication:

2. Instructional routines:

3. Discipline procedures:

4. Independent work:

5. Cooperative learning:

6. Differentiated instruction:

Tool 5.3

7. Data analysis:

8. Planning:

9. Accommodations:

10. Evaluation:

11. Homework:

12. Physical environment:

13. Literacy centers:

14. Other:

Tool 5.3

Responsibilities of Co-Teachers

Co-Teachers:____

Directions: Take a few minutes to look over the list of roles and responsibilities and indicate by placing **I** for individual responsibility and **S** for shared responsibility. Discuss your responses with your co-teacher.

_______ Schedule students

_______ Determine curriculum standards

_______ Write content of lesson plans

_______ Write strategies to enhance lesson plans

_______ Check appropriate course objectives with individual student IEPs

_______ Model behavioral strategies

_______ Determine accommodations

_______ Adapt assessments, materials, class environment

_______ Grade student work

_______ Determine student behavioral expectations

_______ Determine student academic expectations

_______ Monitor and evaluate progress on individualized education program (IEP)

_______ Plan for parent communication

_______ Plan for student conferencing

What other responsibilities can you add?

Tool 5.4

Co-Teaching Instructional Approaches

There are a variety of co-teaching approaches depending on the student and teacher needs, the curriculum content, and the instructional strategies. Co-teaching partners can alternate the roles and approaches regularly and this becomes more fluid as professionals become comfortable with each other in the shared space.

- **Team Teaching:** Both teachers deliver the instruction at the same time. One may write notes on the board while the other speaks; one may model while the other explains; or both may simply take turns delivering the instruction. This may include shared lecturing or a division of responsibilities in presenting instruction. This approach requires the most commitment to planning and a high level of respect and trust for each other.
- **One Teach, One Support:** One teacher may have the primary instructional responsibility, while the other circulates through the room providing unobtrusive assistance to an individual or small group of students. Assistance can include visual cues, verbal prompts, nonverbal reinforcement, monitoring academic behaviors, and refocusing student direction. The teachers could alternate this role.
- **Parallel Teaching:** Both educators plan jointly and teach the same information simultaneously, but they divide the class into two groups. The teachers coordinate their efforts and the students receive the same instructional material.
- **Center or Station Teaching:** The teachers divide the content and students. Each teacher provides direct instruction to one group and subsequently repeats the lesson for the other groups. At the third center, students can be working independently. This approach requires that teachers plan to divide the instructional content and that both have responsibilities for delivering instruction. The students benefit from the lowered teacher-student ratio.
- **Remedial/Enrichment Teaching-Alternative Teaching:** One teacher works with a small group to preteach or reteach a concept or skill while the other provides enrichment or alternative activities for the rest of the class. This approach addresses enrichment and assessment.

Co-Teaching Collaborative Planning

Collaborative planning is an integral component of any co-teaching structure. A co-teaching plan needs to address the in class schedule, co-planning, shared classroom rules, team member responsibilities, student responsibilities and expectations, instructional formats and strategies, and the evaluation process. Administrators can assist by scheduling joint planning periods for co-teachers. Through co-planning, educators jointly identify student needs and curricular objectives. The general education teacher brings expertise with content and curriculum standards, while the special education teacher brings expertise in learning and instructional strategies and

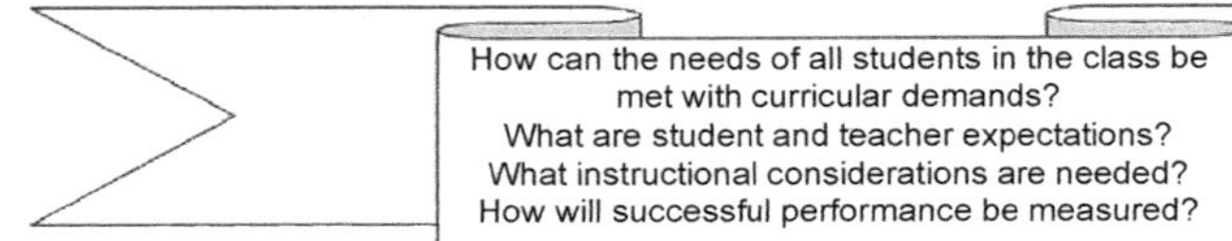

Co-Teaching Lesson Planning Form

Teacher (s): ______________________________________

Subject: ______________________________________

Standard: ______________________________________

____

Objectives: ______________________________________

____

____

Main Instructional Activities	Person Responsible Co-Teaching Approach	Evaluation
Instructional Considerations (preferences/strengths/needs)		

Tool 5.5

Opening Activity (Hook)		
Teacher Activities		
Student Activities		
Closure		

Resources/Materials:

Lesson Reflection:

Tool 5.5

differentiated instruction. Professionals from related services bring knowledge in a particular therapy (speech and language, physical, occupational, assistive technology). Each educator brings unique attributes to the partnership and together they maximize learning of all students. In joint planning, teachers help one another by providing different areas of expertise that, when fused together, can result in enhanced instruction for all students (Murawski & Dieker, 2004).

During the planning phase, co-teaching partners determine the content and student performance outcomes for learning. Instructional formats and strategies, accommodations, and co-teaching approaches are all components of planning. Instructional formats address all students' engagement in the activity or lesson. It can be activity-based, center learning, self-directed, lecture, or paper-pencil tasks. Instructional arrangements can be teacher directed, small or large group, independent work, cooperative group, or remediation.

Co-teaching partners can create co-teaching plans that target the content, resources, strategies, teaching responsibilities and approaches. This plan is influenced by the student population, instructional time, and curriculum/instructional demands. **Tool 5.5, Co-Teaching Lesson Planning Form** (pp. 74–75), exemplifies one way of approaching the planning process. Co-teachers can use this guide to determine the parameters of shared instruction. It is imperative to be flexible and to implement changes based on concerns, ideas, and student needs.

Co-teaching, through ongoing communication and a joint responsibility for problem solving, can offer consistency in instructional delivery for all students based on shared expectations. This plan provides a structure to initiate discussion regarding student and teacher responsibilities and the strategies and approaches that can be used to increase postive outcomes for teachers and students.

An Example of Responsibilities of Co-Teachers:

- **General educator:** determine curriculum plan standards based lessons, develop assessments
- **Special educator:** provide learning strategies, adapt assessments, monitor IEP goals, and develop re-teaching lessons
- **Jointly:** parent contacts, evaluating work, present lessons, develop games and hands on materials for literacy centers

The co-teaching plan and the responsibilities shared between co-teachers can change as teachers' confidence and competence in planning and instruction develops. This plan is a global view of the student and teacher responsibilities.

Tool 5.6, Co-Teaching Strategy Plan (p. 79), is a co-teaching lesson planning form that allows for elaboration of strategic approaches and expectations. **Tool 5.7, Evaluating Co-Teaching Instructional Approaches** (p. 81), allows for reflection and evaluation of approaches used in the co-teaching classroom. Teachers can use the results of this tool for future planning and professional development.

Tips for Planning

- Be flexible.
- Co-plan at least one period a week.
- Review content prior to meeting.
- Use a curriculum map.
- Begin with learning objectives and standards (KUD = Know, Understand, Do).
- Discuss strategies to remediate, enrich and extend the curriculum.
- Utilize ongoing progress monitoring to create strategic grouping.
- Include the co-teaching approaches in plan.
- Adjust plans based on student needs and progress.
- Reflect and evaluate on previous plans.

According to Murawski and Dieker (2004) In joint planning, teachers help one another by providing different areas of expertise that, when fused together, can result in enhanced instruction for all students.

The Evaluation of the Co-Teaching

Continuous evaluation of co-teaching is essential for continued growth of the partnership and improved teaching and learning opportunities for students. It is during the evaluation stage that co-teachers can reflect on the process and outcomes of their hard work and commitment. It is important to invite all partners in the teaching and learning into the evaluation phase. **Tool 5.8, Co-Teaching Rating Scale** (p. 80), is a structure to be completed individually and then discussed together. The tool is intended to be developmental to influence future practices, so honesty is essential. There is a section for additional comments so that co-teachers can discuss other aspects of their relationship.

The **Co-Teaching Rating Scale** can be used periodically as an informal evaluation to examine the co-teaching relationship. The scale will provide information on the specific aspects of the classroom and each participant's view. The co-teachers can compare their scales and use them as a forum for discussion and reflection.

The co-teaching classroom provides a forum for both teachers to take responsibility for all students in the classroom; therefore, having the parents of the students in the classroom evaluate the model can foster additional information about the structure. **Tool 5.9, Parent Co-Teaching Rating Scale** (p. 82), can be used for gathering data regarding the parent's perspective about the co-teaching structure. This can be done at the end of the year to be used for reflection and future planning.

Building a co-teaching relationship involves consultation and collaboration and supports the use of the tools introduced throughout the book for the development and maintenance of an effective partnership. **Tool 5.10, Checklist of Tools for Consultation, Collaboration, and Co-Teaching** (pp. 83–84), provides a list of the tools presented that can be used in all of the structures of consultation, collaboration, and co-teaching. Partnerships can use this to make decisions about what tools they will employ to develop their collaborative work. The selection of tools may vary depending on each collaborative relationship.

Summary

With an increasingly diverse student population and current legislative mandates, classrooms no longer flourish behind closed doors and with single ownership of learning spaces. Co-teaching provides students with disabilities, English language learners, and at-risk students access to the general education curriculum while providing the required accommodations and services. Co-teaching promotes partnerships between professionals that are based on shared teaching and learning practices. The general education teacher brings expertise with content and curriculum standards, while the special education teacher and related personnel bring expertise in strategies and differentiated instruction; together they maximize learning of all students. Developing and nurturing these relationships can assist in meeting the needs of all learners in the general education classroom; therefore, it is imperative to spend time learning about each other's communication style, classroom expectations, and teaching style. Planning and evaluation provide a forum for working together to achieve common goals for all students.

Co-Teaching Strategy Plan

Team members:____________________Subject:______________Week of:__________

	Lesson Activities	Strategy/Approach *OTOS, PT, ST, AT, TT
Pre-Assessment		
Monday	▪ ▪ ▪	
Evaluation		
Pre-Assessment		
Tuesday	▪ ▪ ▪	
Evaluation		
Pre-Assessment		
Wednesday	▪ ▪ ▪	
Evaluation		
Pre-Assessment		
Thursday	▪ ▪ ▪	
Evaluation		
Pre-Assessment		
Friday	▪ ▪ ▪	
Evaluation		

Note: OTOS = One Teach, One Support; **PT** = Parallel Teaching; **ST** = Station Teaching; **AT** = Alternative Teaching; **TT** = Team Teaching.

Source: Reprinted from Hentz S. (2010). By permission

Tool 5.6

Evaluation of Co-Teaching Instructional Approaches

Directions: Reflect on your practice of co-teaching. Put an X in the box that illustrates the frequency of an instructional approach. Write about the success of the approach and/or areas for improvement.

Instructional Approach	Always	Sometimes	Never	What made this approach successful?	What improvements and additional professional development is required to increase the success and/or use of this approach?
Team Teaching					
One Teach, One Support					
Parallel Teaching					
Center or Station Teaching					
Alternative Teaching					

Tool 5.7

Co-Teacher Rating Scale

Name: ______________________________

Directions: Respond to each statement by putting a check mark in the column that best describes your experience. N = Never S = Sometimes A = Always

	N	S	A
1. Classroom rules and routines have been developed jointly.			
2. We co-planned the physical environment.			
3. We use effective verbal and nonverbal communication.			
4. Humor is part of our classroom environment.			
5. Students view us as equal teachers/partners.			
6. Both teachers communicate with the parents.			
7. Teachers are competent with the curriculum content and instruction.			
8. Both teachers present lessons.			
9. Planning is a shared responsibility.			
10. Time is scheduled for planning.			
11. Differentiated instruction is a component of our classroom instruction.			
12. Teachers use data and analysis to plan instruction.			
13. Teachers share in assessment of all students.			
14. Behavior management is a shared responsibility.			
15. Teachers have fun working together.			

Tool 5.8

Parent Co-Teacher Rating Scale

Name: ______________________________

Directions: Respond to each statement by putting a check mark in the column that best describes your experience with your child in the co-taught classroom.

Key: N = Never S = Sometimes A = Always

	N	S	A
1. Teachers sent home communication about the co-teaching model.			
2. I had the opportunity to communicate with both teachers.			
3. Teachers established a home to school communication system.			
4. Both teachers had a positive relationship with my child.			
5. Teachers provided me with strategies for working with my child at home.			
6. My child viewed the teachers as equal partners.			
7. Both teachers were familiar with my child's strengths and weaknesses.			
8. My child uses a variety of strategies for learning.			
9. Teachers shared evaluation results with me.			
10. Students were given the opportunity to work in flexible groups.			
11. I enjoyed working with both teachers in this model of instruction.			
12. I felt comfortable working with both teachers.			
13. There were times scheduled to meet with both teachers.			
14. Behavior management is a shared responsibility.			
15. My child enjoyed being in a classroom with two teachers.			

Tool 5.9

Checklist of Tools

for Consultation, Collaboration, and Co-Teaching

"I'm a great believer that any tool that enhances communication has profound effects in terms of how people can learn from each other, and how they can achieve the kind of freedoms that they're interested in."

Bill Gates

Checklist of Tools for Consultation, Collaboration, and Co-Teaching

Team members:

Date:

Directions: Place a check as a record of the tools completed in your collaborative.

Building the Partnership

___ Communication Checklist (Tool 1.1)

___ All About Me (Tool 1.2)

___ Plan for Group Reflection (Tool 1.3)

___ Personal Leadership Qualities Survey (Tool 2.1)

___ Reflection of Personal Stories (Tool 2.2)

___ Collaborative Roles and Responsibilities (Tool 2.3)

___ Team Effectiveness (Tool 2.4)

___ Conflict Management Profile (Tool 2.7)

___ Qualities of a Collaborator (Tool 3.1)

___ Am I Ready to Co-Teach (Tool 5.1)

___ Teacher Survey of Co-Teaching (Tool 5.2)

___ My Expectations in the Classroom (Tool 5.3)

Planning

___ Collaborative Project Plan (Tool 1.4)

___ Problem Solving Plan (Tool 2.5)

___ Collaborative Team Action Plan (Tool 3.2)

___ Professional Development Needs Assessment (Tool 3.3)

Tool 5.10

___ Checklist of Potential Consultative Partners (Tool 4.1)

___ Circles of Support (Tool 4.2)

___ Request for Student Support (Tool 4.3)

___ Request for Teacher Support (Tool 4.4)

___ Co-Teaching Lesson Planning (Tool 5.5)

___ Co-Teaching Strategy Plan (Tool 5.6)

Implementation

___ Collaborative Activities and responsibilities (Tool 3.4)

___ Audit of Effective Delegation Practices (Tool 3.5)

___ Student Assessment (Tool 4.5)

___ Consultation Plan (Tool 4.6)

___ Consultation Log (Tool 4.7)

___ Checklist of the Consultation Process (Tool 4.9)

___ Responsibilities of Co-Teachers (Tool 5.4)

Evaluation

___ Evaluating the Collaborative (Tool 3.6)

___ Consultation Evaluation (Tool 4.8)

___ Evaluation of Co-Teaching Instructional Approaches (Tool 5.7)

___ Co–Teaching Evaluation (Tool 5.8)

___ Parent Co-Teaching Rating Scale (Tool 5.9)

Tool 5.10

References

Ahearn, E. (2005). Access to the general education curriculum. Project Forum at NADSE, (pp. 2–7). Retrieved from www.nasdse.org.

Barnitt, V. (2006). *Fostering Achievement and Community Together: F.A.C.T. Folio.* Tallahassee, FL: The Florida Department of Education/Florida Inclusion Network.

Bassett, M., Campbell, G., Hirsch, E., Hupfeld, K., & Reichardt R, (2004). *Alternative teacher preparation in Colorado: Moving from experimental to established.* The Alliance for Quality Teaching. Denver, CO.

Bruner, C. (1991). *Thinking collaboratively: Ten questions and answers to help policy makers improve children's services.* Washington, DC: Education and Human Services Consortium.

Covey, S. R. (2004). *The 7 habits of highly effective people* (15th Anniversary ed.). New York, NY: Free Press.

Dillon, R. S. (2007). Respect for persons, identity and information technology. *Gruppendynamik Und Organisationberatung,* 38, 201–212.

Frattura, E., & Capper, C. (2007). New teacher teams to support integrated comprehensive services. *Teaching Exceptional Children,* 39(4), 16–21.

Friend, M. & Cook, L. (2009). *Interactions: Collaboration skills for school professionals.* Columbus, OH: Pearson.

Gately, S. (2005). Two heads are better than one. *Principal Leadership,* 5, 9, 36-41.

Gudwin, D. M., & Salazar-Wallace, M. D. (2010). *Mentoring and coaching: A lifeline for teachers in a multicultural setting.* Thousand Oaks, CA: Corwin.

Hentz, S. (2007). *Teach smart: Practical strategies and tools for educators.* Sarasota, FL: VIEW Inc.

Hentz, S. (2009). Response to intervention: Powerful, practical tools and strategies for implementing RTI through collaborative and co-teaching models. (Seminar Handbook). Sarasota, FL: View Inc.

Hentz S. (2010). Co-teaching for success: Powerful strategies for working together in today's inclusive classrooms. (Seminar Handbook). Sarasota, FL; View Inc.

Howard, M. (2009). *RTI from all sides: What every teacher needs to know*. Portsmouth, NH: Heinemann.

James, W., & Blank, W. (2006). Review and critique of available learning-style instruments for adults. *New Directions for Adult and Continuing Education*, 59, 47–57.

Johnson, S., & Smith, L. (2008). Implementation of response to intervention at middle school: Challenges and potential benefits. *Teaching Exceptional Children*, 40(3), 46–52.

Kenneth W., & Kilmann, R. H. (1999), *Thomas-Kilmann Conflict Mode Instrument*. Palo Alto: CA. Consulting Psychologists Press, Inc.

Lipman, L. (2007). Taking your team to new heights with fun team building. Retrieved from http://www.funteambuilding.com/top10.php.

Marzano, R. J., Pickering, D. J., & Pollock, J. E. (2001). *Classroom instruction that works: Research-based strategies for increasing student achievement*. Alexandria, VA: ASCD.

Murawski, W., & Dieker, L. (2004). Tips and strategies for co-teaching at the secondary level. *Exceptional Children*, 36(5), 52–58.

Newman, D. S. (2007). An investigation of the effect of instructional consultation teams on special education placement rate. Retrieved from http://hdl.handle.net/1903/7772.

Quenk, L. (2000). *Understanding type, stress and inferior function*. Mountain View, CA: CPP, Inc.

Villa, R., & Thousand, J. (2005). Creating an inclusive school. Alexandria, VA: ASCD.

Wilderdom, a project in natural living & transformation (2011). Retrieved from http://wilderdom.com.